HAL•LEONARD

pro vocal
BETTER THAN KARAOKE!

SONGBOOK & 2 SOUND-ALIKE CDs
WITH UNIQUE PITCH-CHANGER™

WOMEN/MEN EDITION
VOLUME 11

SELECTIONS FROM THE MOVIE

BOUBLIL AND SCHÖNBERG'S

Les Misérables

ISBN 978-1-4803-2986-7

ALAIN BOUBLIL MUSIC LTD.

EXCLUSIVELY DISTRIBUTED BY

HAL•LEONARD®
CORPORATION
7777 W. BLUEMOUND RD. P.O. BOX 13819 MILWAUKEE, WI 53213

Visit Hal Leonard Online at
www.halleonard.com

CONTENTS
CD 1

CONTENTS
CD 2

At the End of the Day

Music by Claude-Michel Schönberg
Lyrics by Alain Boublil, Jean-Marc Natel and Herbert Kretzmer

gon-na be hell _ to pay _____ at the end of the day.

Foreman:
At the end of the day, you get noth-ing for noth - ing. __

Sit-ting flat on your butt does-n't buy an - y bread. There are

Workers One and Two:
chil - dren _ back at home, and the chil-dren have got to be fed, and you're

Woman One:
luck - y to be in a job and in a bed. _____

Workers:
And we're count-ing our bless - ings. __

Woman Two:
Have you seen how the fore-man is fum-ing to - day _____

with his ter - ri - ble breath and his wan - der-ing hands? _____

got   to   pay _ your way _____   at the end of the   day.

Now what have we here, lit - tle   in - no - cent   sis - ter? __

Come on,   Fan - tine,   let's   have   all   the   news.

Dear   Fan-tine, you must send us more   mon-ey. Co - sette needs a   doc-tor. There's no time to

lose.   Give that let-ter to me. It is none of your   busi - ness __

with   a   hus-band   at home   and   a   bit   on   the   side.

Is there an - y - one here that can swear be-fore   God she has noth-ing to fear, she has noth-ing to

Slower

hide?

bet she's earn-ing her keep sleep-ing __ a - round, __ and the boss

would-n't like __ it.

Fantine: Yes it's true, there's a child, and the child is my

daugh-ter, __ and her fa-ther a-ban-doned us, leav-ing us flat.

Now she lives with an inn-keep-er man and his wife, and I pay for the child. What's the mat-ter with

that? *Women:* At the end of the day, she'll be noth-ing but trou - ble, __

and there's trou-ble for all when there's trou-ble for one. While we're

earn-ing our dai - ly bread, she's the one with her hands in the but - ter. __ You must

send the slut __ a - way, or we're all gon-na end in the gut - ter. __ It's

us who'll have ___ to pay _____ at the end of the

Foreman:
day. I might have known ___ the bitch ___ could bite. ___ I might have known the cat had claws. ___

___ I might have guessed ___ your lit-tle se-cret. ___ Ah, yes, the vir-tu-ous ___ Fan-

tine, who keeps her-self ___ so pure and clean. ___ You'd be the cause, ___

___ I had no doubt, of an-y trou-ble here-a-bout. ___ You play a vir - gin ___ in the

Girl:
light but need no urg - in' in the night. She's been laugh-ing at you while she's hav-ing her

men. You must sack her to - day.

Freely   **Faster**
Right, my girl. On your way.

Bring Him Home

Music by Claude-Michel Schönberg
Lyrics by Herbert Kretzmer and Alain Boublil

Intro
Slowly, freely

A D Amaj7 D A D Amaj7 D

God on

Verse
Moderately slow

A D Amaj7 D A D

high, _____ hear _____ my _____ prayer. _____
peace, _____ bring him joy. _____

Amaj7 D C#m Bm

___ In _____ my need _____ You _____ have
___ He is young, _____ he _____ is

E E7
rit.

al - ways been there. _____ He is
on - ly a boy. _____ You can

A D Amaj7 D A D
a tempo

young, _____ he's _____ a - fraid. _____
take, _____ you _____ can _____ give. _____

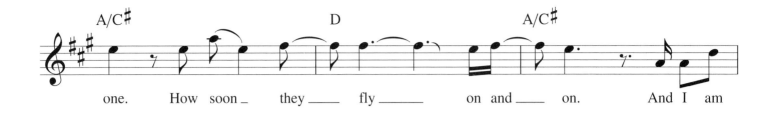

one. How soon _ they ___ fly _____ on and ___ on. And I am

D.S. al Coda

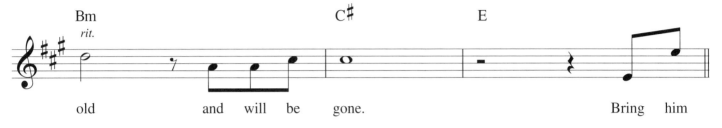

old and will be gone. Bring him

⊕ Coda

Outro

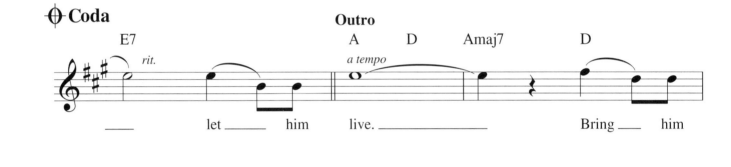

____ let _____ him live. _____ Bring ___ him

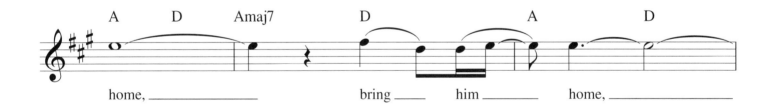

home, _____ bring ___ him _____ home, _____

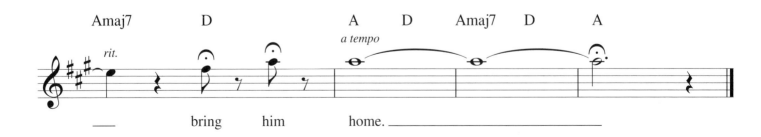

___ bring him home. _____

16

A Little Fall of Rain

Music by Claude-Michel Schönberg
Lyrics by Alain Boublil, Jean-Marc Natel and Herbert Kretzmer

Slower

Verse

Faster

Slower

18

Castle on a Cloud

Music by Claude-Michel Schönberg
Lyrics by Alain Boublil, Jean-Marc Natel and Herbert Kretzmer

Bridge

There is a la - dy all in white, holds me and sings a lull - a - by. She's nice to see and she's soft to touch. She says, "Co - sette, I love you ver - y much."

Verse

I know a place where no one's lost.

I know a place where no one cries.

Cry - ing at all is not al - lowed,

not in my cas - tle on a cloud.

Do You Hear the People Sing?

Music by Claude-Michel Schönberg
Lyrics by Alain Boublil, Jean-Marc Natel and Herbert Kretzmer

(2.) *See additional lyrics*

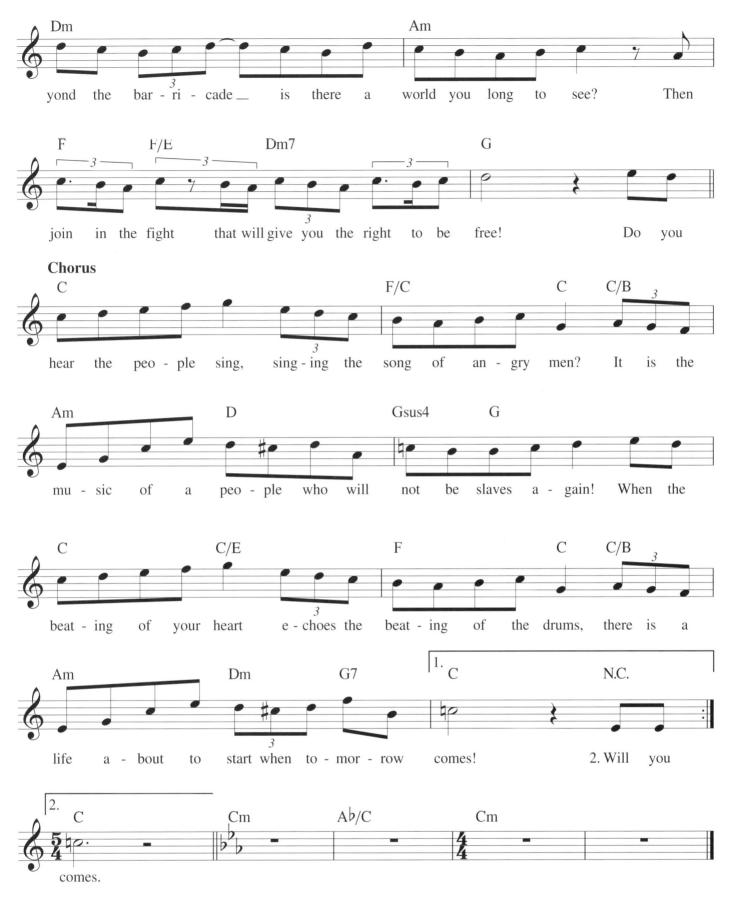

Additional Lyrics

2. Will you give all you can give
So that our banner may advance?
Some will fall and some will live;
Will you stand up and take your chance?
The blood of the martyrs will
Water the meadows of France!

Drink with Me
(To Days Gone By)

Music by Claude-Michel Schönberg
Lyrics by Herbert Kretzmer and Alain Boublil

Empty Chairs at Empty Tables

Music by Claude-Michel Schönberg
Lyrics by Herbert Kretzmer and Alain Boublil

Here it was they lit the flame. _____

Here they sang a - bout to - mor - row, and

to - mor - row nev - er came.

Bridge

From the ta - ble in the

cor - ner they could see a world re -

born. _____ And they rose with voic - es

ring - ing, and I can hear _____ them

now. The ver - y words _____ that they had

A Heart Full of Love

Music by Claude-Michel Schönberg
Lyrics by Alain Boublil, Jean-Marc Natel and Herbert Kretzmer

Co-sette, _____ Co-sette.

This is a chain _ we'll nev-er break. _____

Do _ I dream? A heart full _____ of _

I'm a-wake.

Marius:
_ love, _ a heart full _____ of you, one sin-gle

Cosette:
A heart full _____ of you.

Éponine:
He was nev-er mine _____ to lose. _____ Why _

look and then I knew. _

I knew it too.

_ re-gret what could not be? These are words _

32

Marius: From _ to - day

Éponine: he'll nev - er ____ say, ____ not to me, not to

Outro

Marius: For it is - n't ____ a

Cosette: Ev - 'ry day For it is - n't ____ a

Éponine: me, not ____ for me. His heart full _____ of

dream, not a dream ____ af - ter all.

dream, not a dream ____ af - ter all.

love. He will ___ nev - er feel this way.

33

I Dreamed a Dream

Music by Claude-Michel Schönberg
Lyrics by Alain Boublil, Jean-Marc Natel and Herbert Kretzmer

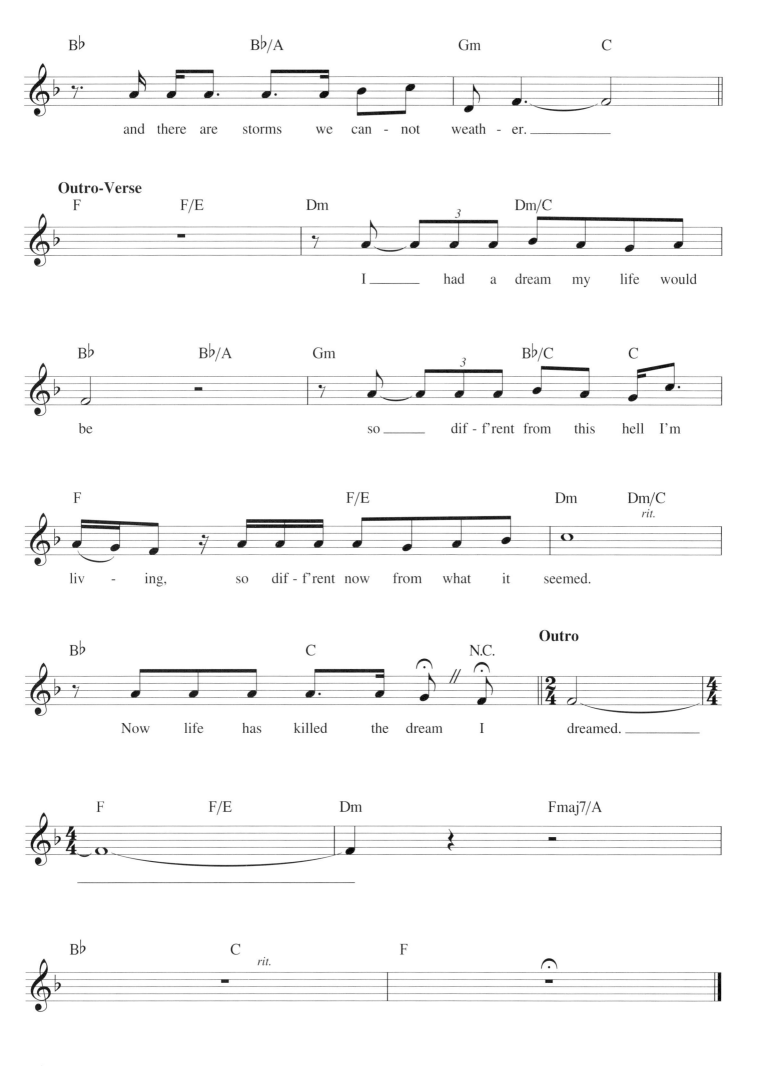

In My Life

Music by Claude-Michel Schönberg
Lyrics by Alain Boublil, Jean-Marc Natel and Herbert Kretzmer

Master of the House

Music by Claude-Michel Schönberg
Lyrics by Alain Boublil, Jean-Marc Natel and Herbert Kretzmer

Chorus

tent to be. Mas-ter of the house, dol-in' out the charm,

read-y with a hand-shake and an o-pen palm. Tells a sauc-y tale,

makes a lit-tle stir, cus-tom-ers ap-pre-ci-ate a bon vi-veur.

Glad to do me friends a fa - vor, does-n't cost me to be nice.

But noth-ing gets you noth - ing, ev - 'ry-thing has got a lit-tle

price. Mas-ter of the house, keep-er of the zoo,

read-y to re-lieve 'em of a sou or two. Wa-ter in' the wine,

mak-in' up the weight, pick-in' up their knick-knacks when they can't see straight.

Chorus

liv-er ___ of a cat, fill-in' up the sau-sag-es with this and that.

Res-i-dents are more than wel - come. _ Bri-dal suite is oc-cu-

pied. Rea-son-a-ble charg-es, plus ___ some lit-tle ex-tras on the

side. _ Charge 'em ___ for the lice, ex-tra ___ for the mice,

two per-cent for look-in' in the mir-ror twice. Here a lit-tle slice,

there a lit-tle cut, three per-cent for sleep-in' with the win-dow shut.

When it comes to fix-in' pric - es ___ there are lots of tricks he

knows. How it all in-creas-es, all ___ them bits and piec-es. Je-

God knows how I've last - ed liv - ing with this bas-tard in the

Tempo I
Chorus-Outro

house. Mas - ter of the house. Mas - ter and a half. _

Him:

Com-fort-er, phi-los-o-pher. Don't make me laugh. Ser-vant to the poor,

Him:

but-ler to the great. Hyp-o-crite and toad-y and in-e-bri-ate.

Him:

Ev-'ry-bod-y bless the land - lord. ___ Ev-'ry-bod-y bless his spouse. _

Ev-'ry-bod-y raise a glass. ___

Her:

Raise it up the mas-ter's ass. ___

Him:

Ev-'ry-bod-y raise a glass _

___ to the mas-ter of the house.

Stars

Music by Claude-Michel Schönberg
Lyrics by Herbert Kretzmer and Alain Boublil

face,   'til we come face to face.

Bridge

He knows his way   in the dark; _____

mine   is   the   way   of   the   Lord. _____

Those who fol - low _____ the path of the right - eous

shall have their re - ward. _____   And if they

fall   as   Lu - ci - fer   fell,   the   flame, _____   the

Verse

sword! _____   Stars,

in your mul - ti - tudes, ___ scarce to be

count - ed, _____ fill - ing the dark - ness _____

___ with or - der and light. You

are the sen - ti - nels, si - lent _____ and sure, ___

keep - ing watch in the night, _____

keep - ing watch in the night. _____

Bridge

You know your place in the sky, _____

you hold your course and your aim, _____

On My Own

Music by Claude-Michel Schönberg
Lyrics by Alain Boublil, Jean-Marc Natel,
Herbert Kretzmer, John Caird and Trevor Nunn

Intro
Moderately slow

And now I'm all a-lone a-gain, no-where to turn, no one to go to. ___

With-out a home, with-out a friend, with-out a face to say hel-lo to.

And now the night is near, and I can make be-lieve_ he's_ here.

Some-times I walk a-lone at night when ev-'ry-bod-y else is

Suddenly

Music by Claude-Michel Schönberg
Lyrics by Herbert Kretzmer and Alain Boublil

Bridge

How was I to know at last __ that hap-pi-ness __ can come __ so fast?

Trust-ing me __ the way __ you do, I'm so a-fraid of fail-ing you.

Just a child __ who can-not know __ that dan - ger fol-lows __ where I go.

There are shad-ows ev-'ry-where and mem-o-ries I can-not share.

Verse

Nev-er-more a-lone, nev-er-more __ a-part,

you have _____ warmed my heart _____ like the sun.

You have brought __ the gift of life __ and love, so long de-nied me. __

Sud-den-ly I see what I could not see.

Outro

Some-thing sud-den-ly has be-gun. __

57

Who Am I?

Music by Claude-Michel Schönberg
Lyrics by Alain Boublil, Jean-Marc Natel and Herbert Kretzmer

B

Must I lie? ____ How can I ev - er face my

G♯m7 **G♯m7/F♯** **E** **E/D♯**

fel - low men? How can I ev - er face my - self a - gain? My

C♯m7 **F♯9**

soul be - longs to God, I know. I made that bar - gain long a - go.

E♭/G **E♭7**

He gave me hope when hope was gone. He gave ____ me

G♯m **G♯m/F♯** **Fm7♭5** **N.C.** **Faster** **B/F♯**

strength to jour - ney on. Who am I?

F♯ **B** **A**

Who am I? I'm Jean Val - jean!

G **F♯** **E♭** **E♭7/G**

And so, Ja - vert, you see it's true, ____ that man bears

G♯m7 **G♯m7/F♯** **Fm7♭5** **N.C.** **B/F♯**

no more guilt than you. Who am I?

F♯ **B**

Two, four, six, oh, one! _____

Pro Vocal® Series

SONGBOOK & SOUND-ALIKE CD
SING GREAT SONGS WITH A PROFESSIONAL BAND

Whether you're a karaoke singer or an auditioning professional, the Pro Vocal® series is for you! Unlike most karaoke packs, each book in the Pro Vocal Series contains the lyrics, melody, and chord symbols for at least eight hit songs. The CD contains demos for listening, and separate backing tracks so you can sing along. The CD is playable on any CD player, but it is also enhanced so PC and Mac computer users can adjust the recording to any pitch without changing the tempo! Perfect for home rehearsal, parties, auditions, corporate events, and gigs without a backup band.

WOMEN'S EDITIONS

00740247	**1. Broadway Songs**	$14.95
00740249	**2. Jazz Standards**	$15.99
00740246	**3. Contemporary Hits**	$14.95
00740277	**4. '80s Gold**	$12.95
00740299	**5. Christmas Standards**	$15.95
00740281	**6. Disco Fever**	$12.95
00740279	**7. R&B Super Hits**	$12.95
00740309	**8. Wedding Gems**	$12.95
00740409	**9. Broadway Standards**	$14.95
00740348	**10. Andrew Lloyd Webber**	$14.95
00740344	**11. Disney's Best**	$15.99
00740378	**12. Ella Fitzgerald**	$14.95
00740350	**14. Musicals of Boublil & Schönberg**	$14.95
00740377	**15. Kelly Clarkson**	$14.95
00740342	**16. Disney Favorites**	$15.99
00740353	**17. Jazz Ballads**	$14.99
00740376	**18. Jazz Vocal Standards**	$16.99
00740375	**20. Hannah Montana**	$16.95
00740354	**21. Jazz Favorites**	$14.99
00740374	**22. Patsy Cline**	$14.95
00740369	**23. Grease**	$14.95
00740367	**25. ABBA**	$15.99
00740365	**26. Movie Songs**	$14.95
00740360	**28. High School Musical 1 & 2**	$14.95
00740363	**29. Torch Songs**	$14.95
00740379	**30. Hairspray**	$15.99
00740380	**31. Top Hits**	$14.95
00740384	**32. Hits of the '70s**	$14.95
00740388	**33. Billie Holiday**	$14.95
00740389	**34. The Sound of Music**	$16.99
00740390	**35. Contemporary Christian**	$14.95
00740392	**36. Wicked**	$17.99
00740393	**37. More Hannah Montana**	$14.95
00740394	**38. Miley Cyrus**	$14.95
00740396	**39. Christmas Hits**	$15.95
00740410	**40. Broadway Classics**	$14.95
00740415	**41. Broadway Favorites**	$14.99
00740416	**42. Great Standards You Can Sing**	$14.99
00740417	**43. Singable Standards**	$14.99
00740418	**44. Favorite Standards**	$14.99
00740419	**45. Sing Broadway**	$14.99
00740420	**46. More Standards**	$14.99
00740421	**47. Timeless Hits**	$14.99
00740422	**48. Easygoing R&B**	$14.99
00740424	**49. Taylor Swift**	$16.99
00740425	**50. From This Moment On**	$14.99
00740426	**51. Great Standards Collection**	$19.99
00740430	**52. Worship Favorites**	$14.99
00740434	**53. Lullabyes**	$14.99
00740438	**54. Lady Gaga**	$14.99
00740444	**55. Amy Winehouse**	$15.99
00740445	**56. Adele**	$16.99
00740446	**57. The Grammy Awards Best Female Pop Vocal Performance 1990-1999**	$14.99
00740447	**58. The Grammy Awards Best Female Pop Vocal Performance 2000-2009**	$14.99
00116334	**61. Taylor Swift Hits**	$14.99

MEN'S EDITIONS

00740248	**1. Broadway Songs**	$14.95
00740250	**2. Jazz Standards**	$14.95
00740278	**4. '80s Gold**	$12.95
00740298	**5. Christmas Standards**	$15.95
00740280	**6. R&B Super Hits**	$12.95
00740282	**7. Disco Fever**	$12.95
00740310	**8. Wedding Gems**	$12.95
00740411	**9. Broadway Greats**	$14.99
00740333	**10. Elvis Presley – Volume 1**	$14.95
00740349	**11. Andrew Lloyd Webber**	$14.95
00740345	**12. Disney's Best**	$14.95
00740347	**13. Frank Sinatra Classics**	$14.95
00740334	**14. Lennon & McCartney**	$14.99
00740453	**15. Queen**	$14.99
00740335	**16. Elvis Presley – Volume 2**	$14.99
00740343	**17. Disney Favorites**	$14.99
00740351	**18. Musicals of Boublil & Schönberg**	$14.95
00740337	**19. Lennon & McCartney – Volume 2**	$14.99
00740346	**20. Frank Sinatra Standards**	$14.95
00740338	**21. Lennon & McCartney – Volume 3**	$14.99
00740358	**22. Great Standards**	$14.99
00740336	**23. Elvis Presley**	$14.99
00740341	**24. Duke Ellington**	$14.99
00740339	**25. Lennon & McCartney – Volume 4**	$14.99
00740359	**26. Pop Standards**	$14.99
00740362	**27. Michael Bublé**	$15.99
00740454	**28. Maroon 5**	$14.99
00740364	**29. Torch Songs**	$14.95
00740366	**30. Movie Songs**	$14.95
00740368	**31. Hip Hop Hits**	$14.95
00740370	**32. Grease**	$14.95
00740371	**33. Josh Groban**	$14.95
00740373	**34. Billy Joel**	$14.99
00740381	**35. Hits of the '50s**	$14.95
00740382	**36. Hits of the '60s**	$14.95
00740383	**37. Hits of the '70s**	$14.95
00740385	**38. Motown**	$14.95
00740386	**39. Hank Williams**	$14.95
00740387	**40. Neil Diamond**	$14.95
00740391	**41. Contemporary Christian**	$14.95
00740397	**42. Christmas Hits**	$15.95
00740399	**43. Ray**	$14.95
00740400	**44. The Rat Pack Hits**	$14.99
00740401	**45. Songs in the Style of Nat "King" Cole**	$14.99
00740402	**46. At the Lounge**	$14.95
00740403	**47. The Big Band Singer**	$14.95
00740404	**48. Jazz Cabaret Songs**	$14.99
00740405	**49. Cabaret Songs**	$14.99
00740406	**50. Big Band Standards**	$14.99
00740412	**51. Broadway's Best**	$14.99
00740427	**52. Great Standards Collection**	$19.99
00740431	**53. Worship Favorites**	$14.99
00740435	**54. Barry Manilow**	$14.99
00740436	**55. Lionel Richie**	$14.99
00740439	**56. Michael Bublé – Crazy Love**	$15.99
00740441	**57. Johnny Cash**	$14.99
00740442	**58. Bruno Mars**	$14.99
00740448	**59. The Grammy Awards Best Male Pop Vocal Performance 1990-1999**	$14.99
00740449	**60. The Grammy Awards Best Male Pop Vocal Performance 2000-2009**	$14.99

00740452	**61. Michael Bublé – Call Me Irresponsible**	$14.99
00101777	**62. Michael Bublé – Christmas**	$19.99
00102658	**63. Michael Jackson**	$14.99
00109288	**64. Justin Bieber**	$14.99

WARM-UPS

00740395	**Vocal Warm-Ups**	$14.99

MIXED EDITIONS

These editions feature songs for both male and female voices.

00740311	**1. Wedding Duets**	$12.95
00740398	**2. Enchanted**	$14.95
00740407	**3. Rent**	$14.95
00740408	**4. Broadway Favorites**	$14.99
00740413	**5. South Pacific**	$15.99
00740414	**6. High School Musical 3**	$14.99
00740429	**7. Christmas Carols**	$14.99
00740437	**8. Glee**	$16.99
00740440	**9. More Songs from Glee**	$21.99
00740443	**10. Even More Songs from Glee**	$15.99

KIDS EDITIONS

00740451	**1. Songs Children Can Sing!**	$14.99

Visit Hal Leonard online at
www.halleonard.com

7777 W. BLUEMOUND RD. P.O. BOX 13819 MILWAUKEE, WI 53213

Prices, contents, & availability subject to change without notice.

0113